EARLY AMERICAN FAMILY

# *Meet the Dudleys*
## in Colonial Times

by John J. Loeper

## BENCHMARK BOOKS

MARSHALL CAVENDISH
NEW YORK

With thanks to the Hyland House and the
Dorothy Whitfield Historical Society, Guilford, Connecticut

Benchmark Books
Marshall Cavendish Corporation
99 White Plains Road
Tarrytown, New York 10591-9001

Text copyright ©1999 by John J. Loeper
Illustrations copyright © 1999 by Marshall Cavendish Corporation
All rights reserved

Illustrations by James Watling
Musical score and arrangement by Jerry Silverman
Map by Rodica Prato
Photo research by Ellen Barrett Dudley
The photographs in this book are used by permission and through the courtesy of:
Kort Frydenborg Productions, Inc.
Printed in Hong Kong
1   3   5   6   4   2

Library of Congress Cataloging-in-Publication Data
Loeper, John J.  Meet the Dudleys in Colonial Times / John J. Loeper.
p.   cm. — (Early American family)
Includes bibliographical references and index.
Summary: Describes what life was like for a typical Connecticut family in 1750,
including details about home, family, clothing, food, chores, and entertainment.
ISBN 0-7614-0841-X (lib. bdg.)
1. Connecticut—History—Colonial period, ca. 1600–1775—Juvenile literature.
2. Connecticut—Social life and customs—Juvenile literature. 3. Dudley family—
Juvenile literature. [1. Connecticut—History—Colonial period, ca. 1600–1775.
2. Connecticut—Social life and customs. 3. Dudley family.] I. Title. II. Series:
Loeper, John J. Early American family.
F97.L64 1999      974.6'02—dc21 97-27962      CIP  AC

# To the Reader

Colonial New England was settled by men and women who came in search of religious and political freedom. The earliest settlers were the Pilgrims of the Massachusetts Bay Colony.

Connecticut was settled in the 1630s. Some settlers came from England and others migrated from the Bay Colony.

This story is about a family who lived in the Connecticut settlement of Guilford. Life was much different then. Most people lived on farms or in small villages. There were few conveniences. Travel was mainly by horseback over narrow dirt roads. Food was cooked over an open fire, and candlelight dispelled the darkness.

Guilford is a real town. The Dudleys really lived there. They have descendants who are raising families of their own today. The Dudley family reaches out to you from another time and place. Let's go now and meet them.

*I*t was five o'clock on a fine May morning. The town of Guilford was silent and deserted. Long shadows crisscrossed the streets, and the first rays of sunshine gilded the rooftops. In a sheltered doorway a gray cat washed one upthrust leg with her tongue. Not far away, in a secluded backyard, a hound dog shook himself awake. From within the trees and hedges an occasional birdsong disturbed the quiet.

Buildings clustered around a large grassy area called the Green. This common area was used by all the villagers. Some even grazed their sheep here.

The morning sun cleared the horizon and

*It was five o'clock on a fine May morning.*

began its climb. Another day in the year 1750 had arrived.

Of all the houses near the Green, none was more impressive than the stone house built by the Reverend Henry Whitfield. Reverend Whitfield was among the founders of Guilford who came from England in July 1639 and purchased the land from the Narragansett in September.

The chief, or sachem, who signed the agreement with the settlers was a woman named Shaumpishuh. In return for the land she received, "12 coates, 12 fathom of wompom, 12 glasses, 12 payer of shooes, 12 hatchetts, 12 paire of stockings, 12 hoes, 4 kettles, 12 knives, 12 hatts, 12 porringers, 12 spoons and 2 English coates." The tract stretched almost ten miles along Long Island Sound. The new owners called the place Guilford after a town in England.

Like most colonial towns throughout New England, the houses of Guilford were scattered here and there in the surrounding woods and fields. The Dudleys lived about a mile from the Green. Their house was a simple country dwelling,

*Reverend Whitfield was among the founders of Guilford who purchased the land from the Narragansett in September.*

a rectangular farmhouse with a central chimney. Two stories tall, it had eight rooms, four upstairs and four down. A steep wooden staircase wound behind the chimney. The house was made of wood, with a cedar shingle roof, and painted with a mixture called Indian red. A red soil purchased from the local Indians was mixed with fish oil and

*A steep wooden staircase wound behind the chimney.*

rubbed into the wood. This protected the wood and gave it a rich red color.

Fields of corn, oats, and wheat surrounded the house. Two tall maple trees stood in front, and a large barn and other outbuildings clustered behind. A large vegetable garden lay between the house and the barn. In the distance rose low hills and outcroppings of rock. From the crest of these hills you could see the waters of Long Island Sound.

John Dudley came to Guilford about 1670. His origins are a mystery. He said that as a young man he had been pressed into service aboard a British man-of-war and made to work as a deckhand. He managed to escape while the ship was in the West Indies and then made his way to Boston. From there he came to Guilford. Some historians claim that he was the grandson of Thomas Dudley, an early governor of the Massachusetts Colony.

After arriving in Guilford, John worked as a farmhand for Thomas French. In a short while he married French's daughter, Martha, and was given twenty acres of land as a wedding present. This made John a "planter," a settler in the new community. He built a house on his land, and he and Martha raised a family of eight children. John and Martha were David Dudley's grandparents. David Dudley is the father of the family we will visit today.

The Dudley family could trace their ancestors back to the tenth century in England. They played important roles in English history and were members of the nobility. There was even a Dudley Castle in England. Aunt Betsy liked to boast, "We were friends and advisors to kings and queens!"

It was still dark when the Dudley children were awakened by their mother. They threw back the covers and groaned at leaving the warmth of their beds. By the time they had dressed and scampered down to the kitchen for breakfast, their father had fed his three horses and tended the chickens and pigs. He had milked the cow and a jug of fresh warm milk sat on the table. Their mother and Aunt Betsy were preparing

*The Dudley children scampered down to the kitchen for breakfast.*

johnnycake and fussing over a kettle of mush,
which bubbled and hissed over the fire.

The family gathered around a big plank table.
Mr. Dudley said the blessing, and there followed
the clatter of pewter spoons in pewter bowls.
After breakfast, Mr. Dudley led his family in
prayer. He was a devout man and a deacon in
the Congregational church. Then the day's
business was discussed.

"David, the barnyard must be cleaned of

manure before you go to school," Mr. Dudley ordered. Thirteen-year-old David acknowledged his assignment with a nod of his head. "Ann and Ruth, you are to help Aunt Betsy in the vegetable garden before you leave the house." Ruth lowered her head and rolled her eyes, thinking no one was looking.

Ann glanced across at her sister and giggled. She remembered the time, not so long ago, when Ruth had pulled out some poison ivy when she was working in the garden. Her hands had turned red and become covered with welts. At mealtime, Ann had spoonfed her like a baby, and David had called her a lobster.

"Mind the poison ivy!" Ann whispered.

Ruth's dark eyes flashed, as she tossed her head. "Should I find any, I shall put it in David's bed!" she snapped.

Mrs. Dudley's attention turned to six-year-old Nathan. He was still finishing the last of his mush.

"And you, young master, are to stop dawdling. Finish your breakfast! Then go upstairs and shake out the quilts."

"We finish spring cleaning today," added Aunt Betsy, smiling at the look of relief on the children's faces.

Mrs. Dudley and Aunt Betsy, like most New England women, believed that a clean house was the mark of a good woman. Two days ago, they had begun cleaning the house from attic to cellar. As soon as Mr. Dudley and the boys helped them empty the downstairs room, they warned the men to stay away from the house.

While Mrs. Dudley scrubbed the soot and grime from the walls, Aunt Betsy washed the windows. Then they coated the walls with whitewash. With a pail of soapy water between them, they got down on their hands and knees to scrub the wooden floorboards. Later they would rub and polish the furniture till it gleamed. And there was still the family's winter clothing to be washed and hung out to dry.

It seemed as if they would never finish. Besides the spring cleaning, the women's days were filled with a never-ending string of household chores. An old saying tells us:

*Two days ago, Mrs. Dudley and Aunt Betsy had begun cleaning the house.*

*Monday for washing,*
*Tuesday for ironing,*
*Wednesday for spinning,*
*Thursday for baking,*
*Friday for cleaning,*
*Saturday for churning,*
*And Sunday for praying.*

Of all the tasks, David disliked washing the most. He had to carry big, heavy pots of water from the well to the house. There the water was

*Of all the tasks, David disliked washing the most.*

boiled at the fireplace. The girls rubbed dirty clothing with homemade soap. They placed the clothes in the pots of boiling water. Broad, smooth sticks, called washing sticks, were used to stir the clothing and lift it out to be rinsed. Woolen clothing was washed in cold water to prevent shrinking. After wringing out the water, the girls hung the washing outside to dry. On rainy days a clothesline was strung across the kitchen and hung with damp sheets and shirts, stockings and towels. The smell of wet, warm wool filled the house.

A thrifty New England housewife, Mrs. Dudley kept all clothing in good repair. She patched faded or worn spots, darned holes in stockings, and secured loose buttons. Except for a few items purchased from the store in town, most clothing was made at home. But, whether bought or made, the Dudleys wore everything for a long time. Clothing was passed down from adult to child, and from child to child. Aunt Betsy's dresses were cut down to fit Ann and then passed on to Ruth, and Mr. Dudley's shirts and trousers were altered to fit David and

Nathan. When an item could no longer be worn, it was cut into pieces that were stitched into patchwork quilts and rag rugs. As an old New England saying goes:

*Use it up, wear it out;*
*Make it do or do without.*

Aunt Betsy took a break from the heavy work of spring cleaning. She climbed the steep stairs to her bedroom and gazed out the window at the fields of her brother's farm. In the distance spread low hills dotted with the white blossoms of dogwood. She watched her brother, David, walk behind the horse and plow.

Working a colonial farm farm required long hours of heavy toil each day. Plowing and seeding were done by hand. Farm tools were heavy and crude. The local blacksmith supplied forks and shovels and plowheads, but they often struck rocks and bent out of shape or broke. As they said in New England:

*From the rising to the setting sun,*
*A farmer's work is never done.*

David Dudley was a good farmer and a kind man. Betsy was unmarried and lived with her brother and his family. She had been given a room in the house in her father's will, where she could stay until she married or died. Besty loved her brother's children as her own.

Betsy had already passed the age when most women married, and she had been certain that she would remain single. But then Byron Ames had entered her life. His wife had died and he lived alone. He often talked with Betsy after Sunday service and finally proposed marriage. Betsy accepted. She liked Mr. Ames very much. Then, to her delight, he told her that he had purchased the farm next to the Dudleys. She could marry and yet stay close to her family. She had confided in her brother and sister-in-law, but had not yet told the children.

"They will be sad at your leaving," Mrs. Dudley told her. "Especially Ruth. She is so fond of you. You are like a second mother."

"What you mean is that Betsy plays and sings with them," Mr. Dudley joked. "She leaves the scolding and discipline to others!"

David Dudley was a good farmer and a kind man.

"Now, David," Betsy replied. "Aunts and grandparents are meant to spoil children."

Betsy loved to sing and to teach the children and their friends new songs. In fact, Mr. Dudley boasted that his sister had the best singing voice in the town. It was Betsy who told the children funny stories about their family and recited folktales and fables that she knew by heart. And Mrs. Dudley had come to depend upon her help in running the house.

In colonial America, each rural household supplied its own needs. Land provided fuel, cloth, and food. Wood from the forests was chopped and stacked for heating and cooking. Wool from sheep was spun into yarn. Flax from the fields became linen shirts and sheets. Wheat was ground into flour, and corn was ground into meal. From gardens came vegetables and from cows came milk and butter. Hens laid eggs, and hogs were butchered to provide ham and bacon. From fruit trees came baskets of apples, plums, cherries, and pears. And there was often a hive of bees in the orchard, whose honey sweetened

*Wool from sheep was spun into yarn.*

cakes, pies, and cookies. Only a few items, such
as coffee, sugar, and spices, were bought at the
Guilford store.

A portion of all fresh food had to be put away
for winter. Meats were smoked and dried to
preserve them. Fruit was turned into jams and
jellies. Cucumbers and beets were pickled in
vinegar. Potatoes and carrots were stored in root
cellars, unheated storage rooms dug out of the
ground.

*A portion of all fresh food had to be put away for winter.*

Out in the field Mr. Dudley stopped plowing to rest awhile, patting his plow horse on the nose as if to compliment him on a job well done. He looked around at the turned earth and took a deep breath. Spring was a time of new beginnings. It was a time to "smell the fields that the Lord hath blessed."

Meanwhile, the children of Guilford were enjoying their first really warm and sunny playtime of the year. Squealing and skipping, laughing and jumping; they celebrated the return of spring after a long and hard winter. Mr. Johnson, the teacher, watched the children's antics with amusement. Since it was such a fine day, he would allow them a few more minutes before calling them to return to their lessons.

Joining hands to form a circle, the children danced round and round, singing a silly rhyme:

> *A farmer went a-trotting,*
> *Upon an old grey mare,*
> *Bumpety, bumpety, bump!*
> *With his daughter there behind him,*
> *So rosey, fat and fair.*
> *Lumpety, lumpety, lump!*

With the last line shouted out, they all fell down. Ruth had hardly caught her breath before she led the others into a second ditty:

> *Here I brew,*
> *Here I bake,*
> *Here I make my wedding cake.*

"Better bake a cake for your Aunt Betsy," one of

the girls taunted Ruth. "My mother says she is sweet on Mr. Ames!"

"That's not true!" Ruth said, stamping her foot.

The school term was almost over. It usually ran from November to May. In the other months, the children helped with planting and tending the fields and with the harvest.

Guilford's first school was founded in 1643. Every Connecticut community with more than fifty families was required by law to have a school, which was public and supported by taxation.

The children's school was built from logs and had a plank floor. The roof was made of roughly hewn shingles, and the interior walls were plastered with a mixture of mud and straw. The school was one large room, with a fireplace to provide warmth in the winter. There were benches for the pupils and a desk and stool for the teacher. Students were divided into groups according to their ability. While Mr. Johnson taught one group, the other students sat at the back of the room, practicing their lessons. The Bible was the main text, although other books

*The Bible was the main text, although other books were used—spelling books, readers, and "arithmetickers."*

were used—spelling books, readers, and "arith-metickers."

Mr. Johnson was the only teacher. He used the "blab" method, in which the teacher gave the lesson and the children repeated it in unison. "Two times two is four," he would say. "Two times two is four," the children would blab.

Everyone walked to school regardless of weather or distance. The Dudley children walked a mile to get there and another mile to go home. In winter they often started off as the morning light was breaking and arrived at a room barely heated by a fresh fire.

Ann and David Dudley were in Mr. Johnson's advanced class. Both could read and write with ease. Ruth and Nathan were in the younger class. Ruth could read from the Bible, but Nathan was just learning the alphabet. Children were not required by law to attend school, but the Dudley children tried to go every day.

Twice a week, Ann Dudley had special permission to leave school before the others. She walked quickly across the Green toward the Congregational Meetinghouse. She had inherited her aunt's singing voice and was on her way to choir practice.

The Congregational church stood at the northwest corner of the Green. It was a large wooden building with a steeple, bell, and clock. The clock had been made and donated by Ebenezer Parmelee. Guilford residents liked to boast that their meetinghouse was the first in

Connecticut furnished with a bell and a clock.

Religion was an important part of life in colonial New England. In every town and village, one of the first public buildings to go up was a church. Then a minister was hired to lead services. The early settlers had left their native land in search of religious freedom. When the founders of Guilford established a church, they said, "We uphold the ordinances of God in a Congregational way."

Each congregation set its own form of prayer and worship. By 1750, there were several Congregational churches in Guilford, but the Dudleys attended the one on the Green.

At home, Mrs. Dudley paused to note the late afternoon sun. She and her sister-in-law had spent the morning and afternoon cleaning, sweeping, and polishing the furniture. They had opened windows and doors to air out musty rooms. What in the world would she do without Betsy? mused Mrs. Dudley. Satisfied that spring cleaning was well on its way, Mrs. Dudley put aside her broom and went to the kitchen

Ann had inherited her aunt's singing voice.

to throw more wood on the fire. It was time to consider the evening meal. School would let out at five, and Mr. Dudley would have worked up a hunger after a day behind the plow.

The kitchen was the heart of the Dudley home. Cooking was done over an open fire. Water was boiled by hanging kettles from hooks. Meat was roasted on an iron rod called a spit, which passed through the meat and rested on brackets over the fire. Potatoes were roasted by wrapping them in wet leaves and burying them in hot coals. Vegetables and beans were baked in Dutch ovens. These cast-iron kettles had long legs that straddled the glowing coals. The Dudley home, like most houses of the period, had a tightly sealed oven—a brick compartment—built right into the chimney. A small fire was lit here to bake breads, cakes, and pies.

Meat and sweets were rare. The only time they were in abundance was on Thanksgiving. Like other New England families, the Dudleys celebrated only one holiday a year and that was Thanksgiving Day, when they gave thanks for the survival of the first settlers in the New

*The kitchen was the heart of the Dudley home.*

World. Thanksgiving was a day above all others. There was always a roasted turkey, plus pies and cakes and cheese and pickles. And Mrs. Dudley served some of her homemade ginger beer. (Christmas would not be celebrated in New England until much later.)

For tonight's dinner Mrs. Dudley would make a stew. She began to drop bits of bacon and salt pork into boiling water. Later she would add cut vegetables to the kettle.

Aunt Betsy breezed into the kitchen, her cheeks flushed with excitement, and deftly tied an apron around her dress as she quietly hummed a tune. She stood on tiptoe, looking into the cupboard for cornmeal and molasses. Earlier today, she had promised the children a special dessert. She would make hasty pudding, Ruth's favorite, which was also quick and easy to make. Betsy had important news to share with the children and wanted the evening to be festive.

*Aunt Betsy would make hasty pudding, Ruth's favorite, which was also quick and easy to make.*

# Hasty Pudding

½ cup of cornmeal
water
salt
butter
½ cup of molasses or maple syrup

*Mix the cornmeal in a bowl with ½ cup of cold water. Pour 1½ cups of water into a saucepan and bring the water to a boil. Add a pinch of salt. Carefully stir in the cornmeal mixture. Cook over a low heat for ten minutes, stirring occasionally. Pour the pudding into a dessert dish. Add a pat of butter and cover with syrup or molasses.*

Ann burst into the kitchen on her way upstairs, but stopped when she saw her mother and aunt. Betsy smiled as she stopped her niece from putting her finger into the bowl of corn-meal.

"How did choir practice go?" she asked.

"We learned a new hymn," Ann replied.

"Sing it for us," Mrs. Dudley said as she stirred the kettle of stew.

Ann began to sing the opening verse: "Confess Jehova thankfully . . . "

"How lovely!" Mrs. Dudley exclaimed. "Perhaps Mr. Dudley will allow you to sing it when we pray together this evening."

The sun was setting in the western sky when the three younger children returned from school. Nathan carried his hornbook. This was a sheet of paper containing the alphabet and the Lord's Prayer, which was fixed to a wooden frame with a handle. The paper was covered with a layer of transparent horn shaved from the discarded antler of a deer. Ruth had her copy of the New Testament, and David held a copy of Aesop's fables. In another week lessons would be over until the next term.

"What happened to your hand?" Mrs. Dudley asked Nathan.

"I just hurt it a little," Nathan replied. He did not mention that he had skinned his knuckles when he tried to grab a slate from the same girl who had taunted Ruth on the playground. On her slate she had drawn a big heart around the names Dudley and Ames.

*A hornbook was a sheet of paper containing the alphabet and the Lord's Prayer, which was fixed to a wooden frame with a handle.*

"He cut his hand while we were playing," Ruth called from the stairs.

"Come here," Mrs. Dudley ordered. "I'll put

*"What happened to your hand?"* Mrs. Dudley asked Nathan.

some comfrey water on it." Nathan held out his hand obediently.

Although Guilford had a practicing physician, Dr. Nathaniel Ruggles, most mothers used homemade remedies to attend to the day-to-day medical needs of their families. They often used herbs—hops, lavender, marigolds, mint, sage, and thyme—for mild complaints. A cold was treated by plunging the feet into very hot water to "draw the cold downward."

"Thank you, mam," said Nathan, as his mother let go of his hand. He was relieved that Ruth had not told the whole story. Aunt Betsy would never marry and leave them!

Colonial families placed a high value on good manners. Courtesy was extended to everyone. Children treated their elders with respect and rarely raised their voices. Families were more formal than they are today. Mrs. Dudley, like most New England wives, addressed her husband as "Mr. Dudley," and he called her "Mrs. Dudley." Given names were seldom used for adults, and children called their father "sir" and their mother "mam."

Yet, along with formality, there was plenty of time for fun. Aunt Betsy helped the girls make cornhusk dolls and showed the boys how to make paper hats. Neighboring women came to the Dudley kitchen to chat. Men came by to borrow a tool or bring news from the village.

People gathered to work together and play games. Women and girls had sewing parties and quilting bees. Men and boys gathered for barn raisings and to pitch horseshoes. "Frolics," as they were called, were usually organized in advance and were always followed by refreshments.

In summer the Dudley family often went to the shore. The children wriggled their bare toes in the sand, while Mrs. Dudley spread out a picnic on a warm, flat rock and enjoyed the cool breezes off Long Island Sound. After a winter snowfall, a moonlit night might find Mr. Dudley hitching the horse to a sleigh. The family bundled up in blankets and headed across the glistening fields,

*Along with formality, there was plenty of time for fun.*

the crunch of trotting hooves and the jingle of sleigh bells breaking the silence.

On other winter evenings, as darkness came

early, the family gathered at the fireside after supper. They listened to Mr. Dudley read from the Bible or they sang hymns. Aunt Betsy entertained them with her stories, too. Unwilling to sit with idle hands, the girls and their mother knitted and sewed as they listened and chatted and sang.

Next to singing with Aunt Betsy, Ann loved to sew, and Ruth was trying her best to keep up with her older sister. Learning to sew was an important part of a girl's education. Before she married, a girl was expected to produce a sample of her sewing skills. Her "sampler" might have the letters of the alphabet or a biblical saying done in a colorful variety of stitches.

The evening meal over, Aunt Betsy brought out her hasty pudding. Nathan and Ruth clapped their hands with pleasure. Betsy paused before saying in a quiet, serious voice, "I have news." She looked at each of the Dudley children in turn.

"Mr. Ames—you know him from church— has proposed marriage, and I have accepted.

*Before she married, a girl was expected to produce a sample of her sewing skills.*

You will have a new uncle. Isn't that wonderful news?"

"No!" Ruth shouted. She started to cry and ran upstairs to her room.

Nathan's eyes widened. His classmate was right. Aunt Betsy was sweet on Mr. Ames!

Ann walked over to her aunt and kissed her cheek. "Never mind about Ruth. She will get over it. I am so happy for you."

"Me, too," David added, trying to conceal any show of emotion.

## To Make a Sampler

*Start with a square of plain cloth. Draw a saying or the letters of the alphabet on the cloth with a pencil. You can add decorations of leaves and flowers.*

*Embroider over your markings with colored thread. Don't forget to sign and date your sampler. Sampler kits with everything you need are available at craft shops.*

"I must go and speak with Ruth," Aunt Betsy told the others. "I must explain to her that I will not be leaving."

"Whatever do you mean?" Ann questioned.

A wide smile crossed Betsy's face. "Mr. Ames has bought the farm that lies just down the road. We will be neighbors."

"How perfect!" Ann exclaimed. "Ruth will be so pleased. And we can keep up with our singing."

Moments later, after speaking with her aunt, Ruth rejoined the family.

"I'm sorry that I ran off like that," she said.

"I thought we were losing Aunt Betsy. But she will be right next door!"

"We had better start thinking of your aunt as Mrs. Ames," Mrs. Dudley broke in.

"She will always be Aunt Betsy to us," Ruth replied.

The table was finally cleared and the dishes washed and put away. Mrs. Dudley, Aunt Betsy, and the girls took up their sewing. Mrs. Dudley had mending to do, and Aunt Betsy had stockings to darn. (This task was put aside during the summer months, when the children went barefoot most of the time and had no need for stockings.) Ann embroidered her sampler, and Ruth practiced her stitches.

After a while, Mr. Dudley announced that it was time for evening prayer. All gathered around while he read from the Bible.

"Your father wants you to sing the new hymn," Mrs. Dudley told Ann.

Clearing her throat, Ann began to sing. Here is the hymn she sang:

# Confess Jehova

Con - fess Je - ho - va thank-ful- ly,    for He is good; for His mer - cie

con - tin - u - eth for - ev  -  er.    To God of gods con - fesse doe ye,

be - cause His boun- ti - ful mer - cie   con - tin - u - eth for - ev  -  er,

Un- to  the  Lord  of  lords con- fess,    be-cause His mer-ci- ful kind - ness

con - - tin - u-eth  for- ev  -  er.    To Him  that doth, Him-self one - ly,

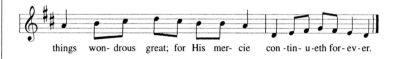

things    won- drous  great; for  His  mer- cie    con -tin- u-eth for- ev - er.

49

*Clearing her throat, Ann began to sing.*

Here are two more verses from the hymn Ann sang:

*To Him that with their firstborn-race*
*Smote Egypt: for His bounteous grace*
*Continueth forever.*
*And Israel bring forth did Hee*
*From mids of them: for, His mercie*
*Continueth forever.*
*With strong hand, and arms stretched-high:*
*Because His bountiful-mercie*
*Continueth forever.*
*To Him that parted the Red Sea*
*In parts: because, His kind-mercie*
*Continueth forever.*

*And caused Israel through to passe*
*Amids it: for, His bounteous grace*
*Continueth forever.*
*And threw Pharoh and his armie*
*In the Red Sea: for His mercie*
*Continueth forever.*
*To Him that in the wilderness*
*Did lead his folk: for His kindness*
*Continueth forever.*
*To Him, that kings of greatness-high*
*Did smite: for, His benigne-mercie*
*Continueth forever.*

Everyone was pleased. Mrs. Dudley had tears in her eyes.

"Will you teach me to sing it?" Ruth asked her sister.

"Of course! Tomorrow we will have a singing lesson. For a change, I will be the teacher," said Ann with a rueful smile and a quick look at her aunt.

The family then joined together in their nightly prayer:

> *Now I lay me down to sleep,*
> *I pray the Lord my soul to keep.*
> *If I should die before I wake,*
> *I pray the Lord my soul to take.*

After the prayer, Aunt Betsy carefully covered the fire with ashes. It would keep until morning, when the coal would rekindle the flames for the next day's use. All of the candles were snuffed except for one, which would light the family on their way to bed. Outside, a bright moon illuminated the fields.

The same moon shone on the Green. Candlelight flickered in a few windows, but most

*Most houses were dark now and families asleep.*

houses were dark now and families asleep.

In the salt marshes around the town, otters and raccoons set out in search of food. Farther inland, deer and rabbits explored the dense forests of oak and evergreen.

The clock in the steeple of the Congregational church marked the hour of ten. Another day in the town of Guilford came to an end.

# Dudley Family Tree

Thomas Dudley marries Dorothy Yorke, 1603, England.

Thomas and Dorothy, Puritan colonists, sail for Massachusetts with John Winthrop. The *Arabella* arrives at Salem, 1630.

Four years later, Thomas Dudley becomes governor of the Massachusetts Bay Colony.

Thomas and Dorothy have 6 children; the eldest, born about 1608, is Samuel.

Samuel (reverend) Dudley marries Mary, daughter of Governor John Winthrop.

Samuel Dudley has 18 children by 3 wives, each of whom dies. Thomas and John, the eldest sons of Samuel and Mary, are raised by their grandfather, Governor Thomas Dudley.

The eldest son, Thomas, is sent to Harvard; John is not. John works for his grandfather, then disappears after his older brother Thomas dies.

In 1670, a John Deadley, or Dudley, arrives in Guilford, Connecticut, from Guilford, Surrey, England.

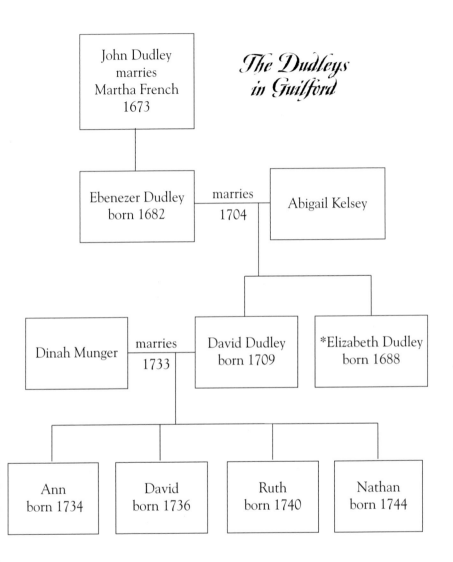

The Dudleys in Guilford

| John Dudley marries Martha French 1673 | | |
|---|---|---|

| Ebenezer Dudley born 1682 | marries 1704 | Abigail Kelsey |

| Dinah Munger | marries 1733 | David Dudley born 1709 | *Elizabeth Dudley born 1688 |

| Ann born 1734 | David born 1736 | Ruth born 1740 | Nathan born 1744 |

*In this story Elizabeth (Aunt Betsy) marries Byron Ames, but in life, she never married.

# Places to Visit

To find out more about how people lived in colonial times, you can visit these museums and restored homes:

**The Griswold Museum**, Guilford, Connecticut
A frame house and restored farm from the 1700s.

**The Hyland House**, Guilford, Connecticut
A typical frame house dating back to 1660.

**Old Deerfield Village**, Deerfield, Massachusetts
Deerfield was laid out in 1666. Many of the early

buildings remain. Much of the village has been
restored.

**The Shelburne Museum**, Shelburne, Vermont
An outdoor museum of thirty-five buildings showing
early American life. Besides houses, there are shops
and craft exhibits.

**The Stone House**, Guilford, Connecticut
The oldest stone house in New England and the
home of Henry Whitfield, a founder of Guilford.

# Books to Read

Many books have been written about life in the New England colonies. Here are some titles you might enjoy:

## Nonfiction

Bracken, Jeanne M. *Life in the American Colonies: Daily Lifestyles of the Early Settlers*. Carlisle, MA: Discovery Enterprises, 1995.

Howarth, Sarah. *Colonial People*. Brookfield, CT: The Millbrook Press, 1994.

Kalman, Bobbie. *Colonial Life*. New York: Crabtree Publishing, 1992.

Perl, Lila. *Slumps, Grunts, & Snickerdoodles: What Colonial America Ate & Why*. New York: Clarion Books, 1979.

Turkle, Brinton, illus. *If You Lived in Colonial Times*. New York: Scholastic, 1992.

Warner, John F. *Colonial American Home Life*. Danbury, CT: Watts, Franklin, 1993.

## Fiction

Bulla, Clyde R. *Charlie's House*. New York: Knopf for Young Readers, 1993.

Butters, Dorothy G. *The Bells of Freedom*. Magnolia, MA: Peter Smith, 1984.

Karr, Kathleen. *Phoebe's Folly*. New York: Harper-Collins, 1996.

# *Index*

Page numbers for illustrations are in boldface.

# About the Author

J. Loeper was born in Ashland, Pennsylvania. He has been a teacher, counselor, and school administrator. He has both taught and studied in Europe.

Mr. Loeper has contributed articles and poems to newspapers, journals, and national magazines. He is the author of more than a dozen books for young readers, all dealing with American history, and an active member of several historical societies. The *Chicago Sun* called him the "young reader's expert on Americana."

Mr. Loeper is also an exhibiting artist and has illustrated one of the books he authored. He and his wife divide their time between Connecticut and Florida.